Feeling Sad

by Helen Frost

Consulting Editor: Gail Saunders-Smith, Ph.D.

Consultant: Erik Willcutt, Ph.D.
Child Clinical Psychologist
Instructor, University of Denver

Pebble Books

an imprint of Capstone Press
Mankato, Minnesota

Pebble Books are published by Capstone Press
151 Good Counsel Drive, P.O. Box 669, Mankato, Minnesota 56002
http://www.capstone-press.com

1 2 3 4 5 6 06 05 04 03 02 01

Library of Congress Cataloging-in-Publication Data
Frost, Helen, 1949–
    Feeling sad/by Helen Frost.
    p. cm.—(Emotions)
    Includes bibliographical references and index.
    Summary: Simple text and photographs describe and illustrate the feeling of
sadness and tell how to alleviate it.
    ISBN 0-7368-0670-9
    1. Sadness in children—Juvenile literature. [1. Sadness.] I. Title. II. Emotions
(Mankato, Minn.)
BF723.S15 F76   2001
152.4—dc21   00-023787

Note to Parents and Teachers

The Emotions series supports national health education standards related to interpersonal communication and expression of feelings. This book describes and illustrates the feeling of sadness. The photographs support emergent readers in understanding the text. The repetition of words and phrases helps emergent readers learn new words. This book also introduces emergent readers to subject-specific vocabulary words, which are defined in the Words to Know section. Emergent readers may need assistance to read some words and to use the Table of Contents, Words to Know, Read More, Internet Sites, and Index/Word List sections of the book.

Table of Contents

4

Sadness is
an unhappy feeling.

Everyone feels
sad sometimes.

You might feel sad
if a friend moves.

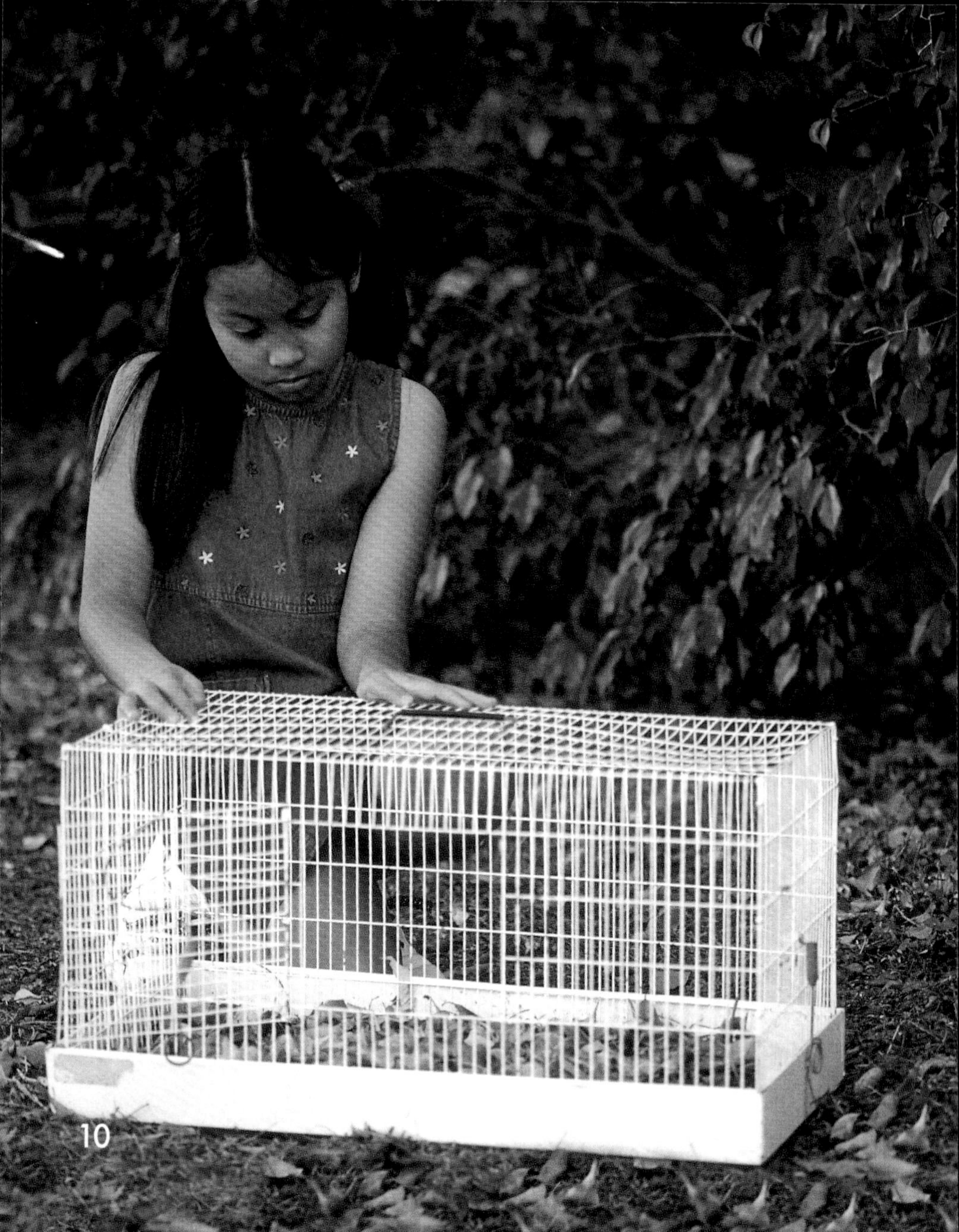

You might feel sad
if your pet dies.

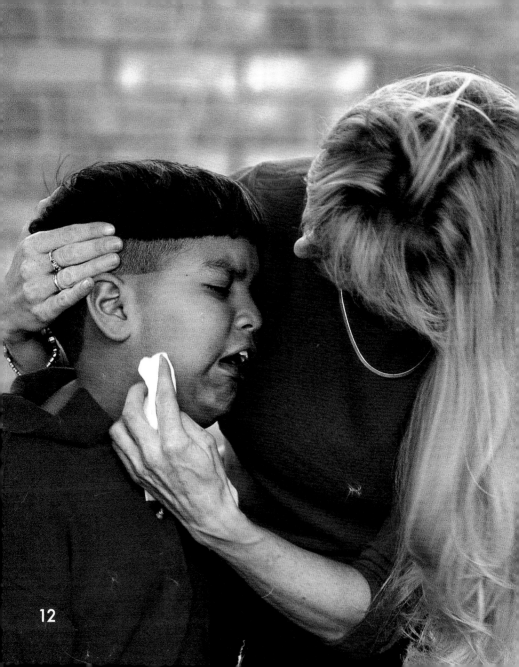

You might cry
when you are sad.

You might want to be alone when you are sad.

You can talk
about your feelings.

You can think
about happy times.

You will see that
sadness can go away.

Words to Know

cry—to weep tears; feeling sad can make people cry; crying sometimes helps people feel better.

feeling—an emotion; sadness is one kind of feeling; some other feelings are anger, happiness, and fear.

sadness—an unhappy or troubled feeling

Read More

Aaron, Jane. *When I'm Sad.* New York: Golden Books, 1998.

Doudna, Kelly. *I Feel Sad.* How Do You Feel? Minneapolis: Abdo Publishing, 1999.

Helmer, Diana Star. *Let's Talk about Feeling Sad.* The Let's Talk Library. New York: PowerKids Press, 1999.

Romain, Trevor. *What on Earth Do You Do When Someone Dies?* Minneapolis: Free Spirit Press, 1999.

Internet Sites

Children's Feelings
http://www.ee.liverpool.k12.ny.us/EE/staff/psychologist/feel.html

Dealing with Feelings
http://www.KidsHealth.org/kid/feeling/index.html

Dealing with Sadness and Loss
http://www.nncc.org/Guidance/dc15_deal.sad.loss.html

Index/Word List

Word Count: 62
Early-Intervention Level: 5

Editorial Credits
Mari C. Schuh, editor; Kia Bielke, designer; Katy Kudela, photo researcher

Photo Credits
David F. Clobes, 8, 14, 18, 20
David Stover/Pictor, 4
Kim Stanton, 1, 6, 16
Marilyn Moseley LaMantia, 10, 12
Scott Barrow/International Stock, cover

The author thanks the children's section staff at the Allen County Public Library in Fort Wayne, Indiana, for research assistance.